America's
ANIMAL
COMEBACKS

Florida Panthers

Struggle for Survival

by William Caper

Consultant: Mark Lotz
Panther Biologist
Florida Fish and Wildlife Conservation Commission

BEARPORT

PUBLISHING

New York, New York

Credits

Cover and Title Page, © Dennis Hallinan/Alamy; 4, Mark Lotz, Florida Fish & Wildlife Conservation Commission; 5, © Thomas & Pat Leeson/Photo Researchers, Inc.; 7, Mark Lotz, Florida Fish & Wildlife Conservation Commission; 8, © Erwin & Peggy Bauer/Wildstock; 9, © Klaus-Peter Wolf/imagebroker/Alamy; 10, © Bill Terry/Grant Heilman Photography; 11, © Gail M. Shumway/BCIUSA; 12, © Lynn Stone/Animals Animals-Earth Scenes; 13A, Mark Lotz, Florida Fish & Wildlife Conservation Commission; 13B, Mark Lotz, Florida Fish & Wildlife Conservation Commission; 14, Mark Lotz, Florida Fish & Wildlife Conservation Commission; 15, Mark Lotz, Florida Fish & Wildlife Conservation Commission; 16–17, © Erwin & Peggy Bauer/Wildstock; 18, © Erwin & Peggy Bauer/Wildstock; 19, Mark Lotz, Florida Fish & Wildlife Conservation Commission; 20, Mark Lotz, Florida Fish & Wildlife Conservation Commission; 21, Mark Lotz, Florida Fish & Wildlife Conservation Commission; 22, © Lynn Stone/Animals Animals-Earth Scenes; 23, © Courtesy of USGS; 25, © Amy Dunleavy; 26, © David S. Maehr; 26 Inset, © Lisa James/Shutterstock; 27, © Daniel J Cox/Natural Exposure; 28, © Lynn M. Stone/Nature Picture Library/Alamy; 29T, © Ruth Cole/Animals Animals-Earth Scenes; 29B, © BIOS Klein & Hubert/Peter Arnold, Inc.; 31, © David Osborn/Alamy.

Publisher: Kenn Goin
Editorial Director: Adam Siegel
Creative Director: Spencer Brinker
Photo Researcher: Amy Dunleavy
Cover Design: Dawn Beard Creative

Library of Congress Cataloging-in-Publication Data

Caper, William.
  Florida panthers : struggle for survival / by William Caper.
      p. cm. — (America's animal comebacks)
  Includes bibliographical references and index.
  ISBN-13: 978-1-59716-532-7 (library binding)
  ISBN-10: 1-59716-532-8 (library binding)
  1. Florida panther—Conservation—Juvenile literature. I. Title.

  QL737.C23C344 2008
  599.75′24—dc22

                                    2007014797

For more information, write to Bearport Publishing Company, Inc., 101 Fifth Avenue, Suite 6R, New York, New York 10003. Printed in the United States of America in North Mankato, Minnesota.

122009
111709CG

1 0 9 8 7 6 5 4 3

Contents

Silence in the Woods

Biologist Mark Lotz can still remember the moment. He had just let a **cougar** run free into the wild. "There was no sound. You're standing ten feet [3 m] away, watching the cougar run into the woods. And you don't hear anything. It's amazing how silent they can be."

This Texas cougar was let loose in the Florida woods.

Perhaps just as amazing was what Mark Lotz was trying to do. In 1995, he and other biologists released eight wild Texas cougars into the woods of southern Florida. It was part of a **bold experiment** to save another animal—the Florida panther. If the plan failed, there might soon be no Florida panthers left in the world.

The Florida panther is a type of cougar. There are 32 kinds of cougars.

Once a Common Cat

Florida panthers were not always in danger of dying out. Until the 1800s, these wild cats lived throughout the southeastern United States. Other kinds of cougars roamed freely in the rest of the country.

Where Florida panthers lived

This map shows where Florida panthers lived before the 1800s. Although this animal is called the Florida panther, it once roamed through many other southeastern states.

As many as 1,360 Florida panthers may have once lived in Florida. No one knows for sure. The animals are shy and very quiet. They live alone and usually hunt at night. As a result, it is hard to find and count them.

The color of the Florida panther's fur helps it blend in and hide.

Panthers and People

In the early 1800s, life became difficult for the Florida panther. Many people **settled** in the southeastern United States. They cleared land and built farms. Settlers now lived in panther **territory**. People feared that the wild cats would attack them and their farm animals.

The panther's skill at being quiet makes it a good hunter. The animal is able to sneak up on and kill the wild hogs and deer that it likes to eat.

Panthers don't hunt people. However, they will hunt farmers' **livestock**, such as sheep, goats, and calves. Early settlers who raised these animals hated the panther. They began shooting the big cats to protect their livestock.

In 1832, **bounties** were set to pay people who killed the feared animal. Now even more people were hunting the Florida panther.

Panthers are most active at dawn and just before the sun goes down. During the day, they can often be found relaxing in the shade.

In 1887, Florida state officials set the bounty for one panther skin at five dollars.

9

Crowded Out

Many **pioneers** moved across the American West in the 1800s. They built homes and ranches on the land. This did not harm the cougars that lived there, however. There was a lot of open space. When people moved into cougar territory, the animals could find new places to live and hunt.

Cougars are skilled hunters. They capture animals by sneaking up on them and attacking suddenly.

Florida panthers living in the Southeast were not so lucky. There was less open space there. When people took over the panthers' **habitat**, it was harder for the cats to find new land. The Florida panther was forced to live in a smaller and smaller area. Soon the animal was found in only one state—Florida.

Panthers need to live in a large area in order to find enough **prey**. Male panthers need about 150–200 square miles (388–518 sq km). Female panthers need about 75–90 square miles (194–233 sq km).

Florida panthers can leap as far as 20 feet (6 m) to attack an animal.

More People, Fewer Panthers

Since the 1830s, the number of people living in Florida has grown quickly. The **population** has doubled almost every 20 years. People have taken over more of the panthers' land. By the 1950s, the wild cats lived only in a small part of southwestern Florida.

In 1958, the Florida government banned panther hunting. In 1967, the U.S. government listed the Florida panther as **endangered**.

As their habitat shrank, so did the number of panthers living there. The animals became separated from other kinds of cougars. The Florida panthers now **mated** only with the few other Florida panthers that lived close by. Over the years, this **inbreeding** caused the animals to become different from other cougars. The Florida panthers began to have kinks in their tails. They now had **cowlicks** on their backs.

A cowlick on the back of a Florida panther

Florida panthers have a kink at the ends of their tails.

Inbreeding Problems

Did inbreeding cause only differences in the way panthers looked? In 1981, scientists began studying Florida panthers to find out. First, they captured the big cats. After examining them, scientists placed **radio collars** around their necks. Then the panthers were set free. Scientists could now track the collared panthers in their natural habitat. As they studied the animals, scientists learned some upsetting things.

Florida panthers do not spend a lot of time in trees. However, they will climb a tree to escape scientists who are trying to capture them in order to fit them with a radio collar.

Mark Lotz and other biologists discovered that inbreeding made Florida panthers more likely to get diseases. Many were born with heart problems that could kill them. Even worse, some inbred panthers had trouble having young. Some could not **reproduce** at all.

Biologists use drugs to make a panther go to sleep so that they can put a radio collar on the cat. Between 1981 and 2007, biologists have used radio collars to study 154 panthers.

Mark Lotz and a panther with a radio collar

Help from Texas

By 1995, only about 30 to 50 Florida panthers were still alive. The animal was almost **extinct**. So Mark Lotz and other Florida biologists came up with a plan to try and save the endangered panther.

Before the Florida panther population became small and separated from Texas cougars, the two animals used to mate with each other.

The scientists knew that there was less inbreeding among the cougars living in Texas. As a result, they were healthier than the Florida panthers. Maybe the Texas cougars and the Florida panthers could have young together. Then the newborn panthers might be healthy.

Texas cougars look very similar to Florida panthers. These Texas cougars live in the wild in Texas.

A Bold Experiment

Scientists had never tried mixing cougar populations before. Mark and the other biologists didn't know if their plan would work. The Texas cougars might not be able to adjust to their new habitat. The land and the **climate** would be a little different from their Texas home. Even if they did adjust, the Florida panthers might kill them. People might kill them, too.

A Texas cougar taking care of her kitten in Texas

18

Before releasing the Texas cougars, biologists put radio collars on them. Scientists could then track the animals to see how they were doing.

In 1995, eight female Texas cougars were set free in the woods where Florida panthers lived. Would they be able to save the panthers from extinction?

One person in Texas caught the eight female cougars that were released in Florida. It wasn't easy. The animals can run short distances at 35 miles per hour (56 kph).

A Texas cougar in Florida with a radio collar

The Experiment Pays Off

By 1996, the biologists' wait was over. Two of the Texas cougars had kittens. They had mated with Florida panthers—and the kittens were healthy!

Panthers give birth to between one and four kittens at a time.

The Florida panther is the most endangered animal in the state.

Mark and the other biologists who had released the cougars were very happy. "It was really great to see that the panthers' health problems could be corrected so easily and quickly," Mark said.

The biologists' plan was working. They had succeeded in making newborn Florida panthers healthier. These cats would be able to have young. The biologists had taken a big step toward helping the panthers survive.

Mark Lotz with Florida panther kittens

A Safe Home

Making Florida panthers healthier was only one part of the challenge facing biologists. If the endangered animal was going to survive, it needed a safe place to live, too. Biologists had already begun to work on that.

In 1982, Florida schoolchildren voted to pick the state animal. The students chose the Florida panther.

In 1989, the U.S. Fish and Wildlife Service established the Florida Panther National Wildlife **Refuge**. Panthers can live safely in its 26,400 acres (10,684 hectares). There are plenty of animals in the refuge for the panthers to hunt. The wild cats can also rest and raise their young there.

The refuge has no fences. Panthers can leave the shelter at any time. However, while they are there, they have a safe and healthy home.

The Florida Panther National Wildlife Refuge is home to water birds and rare flowers as well as Florida panthers. It is located 20 miles (32 km) east of Naples, Florida.

The Florida Panther Today

Today, biologists believe there are about 100 Florida panthers. Their numbers are slowly increasing. However, the cat is still considered one of the most endangered animals in the world.

Habitat loss remains one of the biggest threats facing panthers. People are using more and more land for houses, farming, and businesses. As a result, there is less space for the endangered animal.

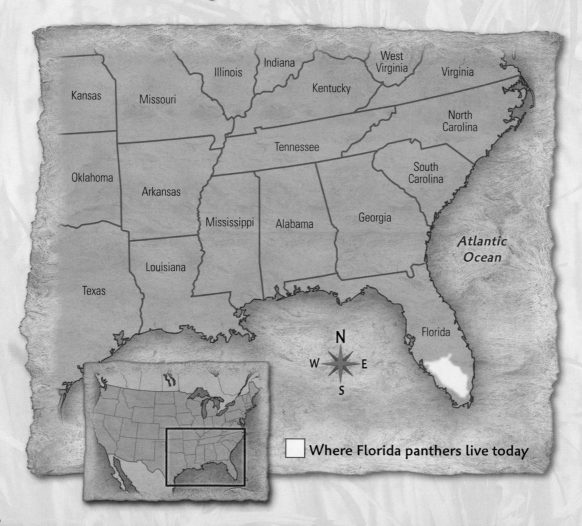

Where Florida panthers live today

As more panthers are born, they need more places to live. Not every panther lives in a park or refuge. If panthers expand their territory, it is more likely they will come into contact with humans. Even people who want to save the Florida panther don't always want one living near their house.

In Florida, special license plates help raise money that is used to protect the Florida panther.

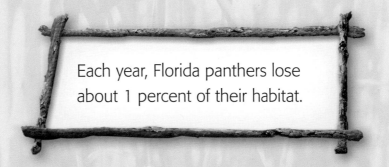

Each year, Florida panthers lose about 1 percent of their habitat.

The Future

People continue to find ways to help the Florida panther. For example, cars sometimes hit panthers that are trying to cross highways. So **underpasses** were built below some roads. The endangered animal can now safely cross under the busy highways.

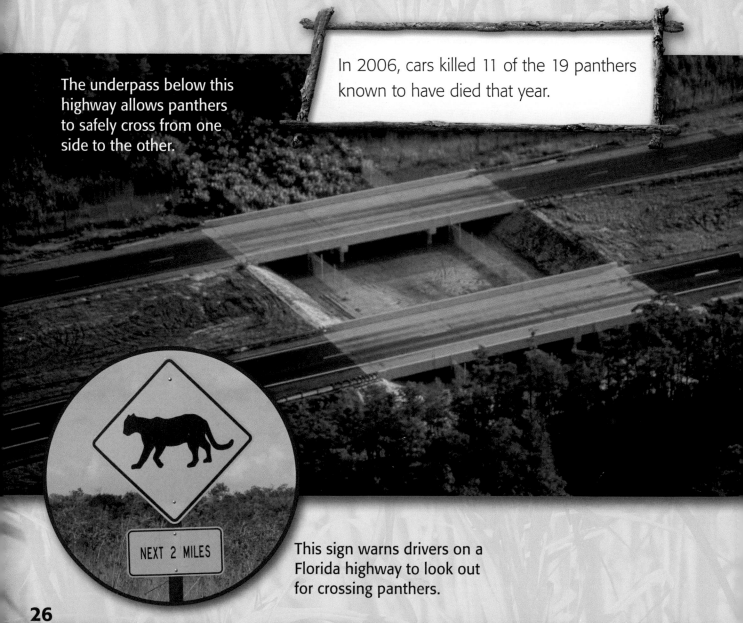

The underpass below this highway allows panthers to safely cross from one side to the other.

In 2006, cars killed 11 of the 19 panthers known to have died that year.

This sign warns drivers on a Florida highway to look out for crossing panthers.

NEXT 2 MILES

The Florida panther's future is still not certain. Biologist Darrell Land warns, "We shouldn't act like the job is done. We've still got a long way to go." Yet today there is more hope than ever for the big cat's survival.

Florida Panther Facts

In 1973, Congress passed the Endangered **Species** Act. This law protects animals and plants that are in danger of dying out in the United States. Harmful activities, such as hunting, capturing, or collecting endangered species, are illegal under this act.

The Florida panther was one of the first species listed under the Endangered Species Act. Here are some other facts about the Florida panther.

Population: **Population in Florida before 1800:** perhaps as many as 1,360

Population in Florida today: about 100

Weight
males: 100–154 pounds (45–70 kg)
females: 55–110 pounds (25–50 kg)

Length
about 7 feet (2 m), including the tail

Height
about 2.5 feet (.8 m) at the shoulder

Fur Color
golden brown

Food
mainly deer and wild hogs; will also hunt armadillos and raccoons

Habitat
southwestern Florida

Life Span
10–15 years

Other Cat Family Members in Danger

The Florida panther is one kind of animal in the cat family that's making a comeback by increasing its numbers. Other members of the cat family are also trying to make a comeback.

Texas Ocelot

- There are fewer than 250 adult Texas ocelots in the world.

- They live in Texas, Arizona, and Mexico.

- Loss of habitat and being hit by vehicles are the main threats to this animal.

- Texas ocelots also face health problems that result from inbreeding.

Snow Leopard

- There are fewer than 2,500 snow leopards in the world.

- They live in eastern Asia.

- Lack of prey and hunting by people are the main threats to this animal.

- Snow leopards are hunted by people for their bones and fur.

Glossary

biologist (bye-OL-uh-jist) a scientist who studies plants or animals

bold (BOHLD) daring

bounties (BOUN-teez) rewards offered for the capture of a harmful animal or person

climate (KLYE-mit) the typical weather in a place

cougar (KOO-gur) a large wild cat that lives in North and South America

cowlicks (KOU-liks) sections of hair that grow in a different direction than the hair around them and which do not lie flat

endangered (en-DAYN-jurd) being in danger of dying out

experiment (ek-SPER-uh-ment) a scientific test set up to find the answer to a question

extinct (ek-STINGKT) when a kind of plant or animal has died out; no more of its kind is living anywhere in the world

habitat (HAB-uh-*tat*) a place in nature where a plant or animal normally lives

inbreeding (IN-*breed*-ing) the mating of closely related individuals

livestock (LIVE-*stok*) animals, such as sheep, chicken, or cows, that are raised on a farm or ranch

mated (MATE-id) came together to have young

pioneers (*pye*-uh-NEERZ) the first people to live in a new area

population (*pop*-yuh-LAY-shuhn) the total number of people living in a place

prey (PRAY) animals that are hunted or caught for food

radio collars (RAY-dee-oh KOL-urz) collars that send out radio signals and are put on animals so that their movements can be tracked

refuge (REF-yooj) a place that provides protection

reproduce (*ree*-pruh-DOOSS) to have young

settled (SET-uhld) made a home and lived in a new place

species (SPEE-sheez) groups that animals are divided into, according to similar characteristics; members of the same species can have offspring together

territory (TER-uh-*tor*-ee) an area of land where an animal lives

underpasses (UHN-dur-*pass*-iz) roads that go below highways

Bibliography

Maehr, David S. *The Florida Panther: Life and Death of a Vanishing Carnivore.* Washington, D.C.: Island Press (1997).

www.bigcatrescue.org/florida_panther.htm

www.fws.gov/floridapanther/

www.myfwc.com/panther

www.panthersociety.org/

Read More

Becker, John E. *The Florida Panther.* San Diego, CA: KidHaven Press (2003).

Clark, Margaret Goff. *The Endangered Florida Panther.* New York: Cobblehill Books (1993).

Silverstein, Alvin and Virginia, and Laura Silverstein Nunn. *The Florida Panther.* Brookfield, CT: The Millbrook Press (1997).

Stone, Lynn M. *Cougars.* Minneapolis, MN: Lerner Publications (1999).

Learn More Online

To learn more about Florida panthers, visit
www.bearportpublishing.com/AnimalComebacks

Index

About the Author

William Caper has written books about history, science, film, and many other topics. He lives in San Francisco with his wife, Erin, and their dog, Face.